Starting Points

Project Ideas for CDT, Science and Technology

John Poole and Jim Sage

MACMILLAN
EDUCATION

First published 1987

Published by
MACMILLAN EDUCATION LTD
Houndmills, Basingstoke, Hampshire RG21 2XS
and London
Companies and representatives
throughout the world

Designed by John Brennan
Typeset by Activity Ltd, Salisbury, Wilts

Printed in Hong Kong

British Library Cataloguing in Publication Data
Poole, John
Starting points: project ideas for CDT, science and technology.
1. Design
I. Title   II. Sage, Jim
745.4   NK1510
ISBN 0–333–40723–7

Contents

▷

More complex projects

Appendix: Reference material

Introduction

The project ideas presented in this book relate to problems that can be solved by *designing* and *making*. They do not include the type of project that is a literature survey followed by copying sections from various books and magazines. The projects in this book can be used with a wide variety of students and situations; they will be found appropriate to courses in science, technology and CDT.

The quality of solutions produced will depend on the age and ability of the students and the time allocated for completion of the project. The time needed will be between 10 and 15 hours for the short structured projects and 30 hours or more for the more open-ended projects. We do give suggested timescales for the various ideas but these should be viewed as being very flexible, since a 10- to 15-hour project can often form the basis of a longer project.

The short structured projects should be used to introduce students to this type of project work. In these projects there are generally only a very few parameters to consider. The longer projects are more open-ended and should be used when students have acquired the appropriate techniques.

All of the projects are multi-disciplinary and although they are often written with particular areas in mind, we do not feel that it is advisable to state them as this would encourage the student to adopt a 'blinkered' approach in solving the problem.

Project work can, if well guided, inspire, excite and motivate students to unexpected levels of achievement, and stretch academically able pupils to their limit. However, this will only happen if the teacher is well organised, shows enthusiasm for the work, is respected by the students and develops a good working relationship with them. This relationship can be achieved through the joint learning situation demanded by project work, enabling the teacher to talk *with* the students, not *at* them, thus assisting the development of mutual respect and trust.

Teachers' notes

Aims of project work

1. To stimulate students and to help them to expand and increase their experience, knowledge and skills, in a motivating way activated by their own interests.

2. To develop a wide range of problem-solving skills.

3. To encourage good working relationships between students and teachers.

4. To make students aware of interactions between technology, society and industry.

Guiding students in project work

The notes below are written in conjunction with the *Students' notes* which follow. Students should be directed to read those before starting their projects and to refer back to them at different stages (see page xi).

When guiding students through project activities the following points should be emphasised:

1. You should direct students to identify possible ideas for projects as early as possible and to discuss them with you. Students will often think of highly motivating projects which are too complex and not achievable in the available time. In such cases it is best to advise the student to consider just one or two aspects of the overall problem. For example, the student might propose, for a 30-hour project: 'Design and make the most energy-efficient boat which is to carry four people and to be motor-driven'. Here the teacher could maintain the student's interest by suggesting that in the time allowed it would be best to investigate only the most efficient shape of hull for such a boat. Model hulls could then be designed and made, and their resistance to forward motion tested in a water tank using a specific model engine.

   The project selected should reflect the student's known ability: it should be formulated so that there is a reasonable chance of a successful solution in the time available. Weaker students can be directed to investigate one or two parameters of a complex problem. This does not remove their initial interest and enthusiasm, but it does make it much less likely that these will quickly evaporate through failure.

2. The project and final report should be started with a clear and concise description of the problem, together with the time in which it is to be achieved.

3. If the project is to be completed successfully, it is essential to plan carefully the use of the available time. Severe time limitations should be highlighted.

4. Suggest that students make a flow diagram of organisation. This will help them to ensure that materials, components, equipment, resources and facilities will be available when and where they are needed.

▷

5   Students should be encouraged to keep a diary of activities, and to develop a portfolio of ideas that will indicate the ability of the student to communicate by a wide range of graphical skills.

       Both of these will be invaluable to students when they prepare their final project report.

6   Students should be encouraged to communicate with outside bodies (such as industry) as appropriate, both when researching aspects of the project and when making the final evaluation.

7   At least three outline solutions to a problem should be produced. A clear process for selecting which solution is to be developed should be indicated, with reasons to justify the choice.

8   *Quantitative* as well as *qualitative* techniques should be used when analysing and evaluating. Students will need to be directed to particular aspects of their project where quantitative work is appropriate.

9   Use block diagrams to display analysis. Students will often find this process easier if they are encouraged to start with the first and last blocks, and then to fill in the intermediate blocks.

       For example, a car-parking system might look like this:

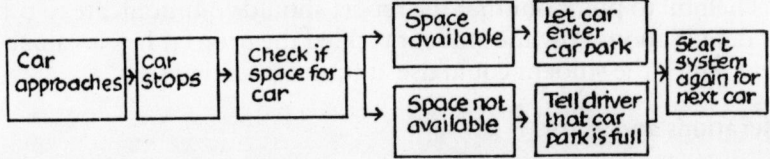

10   All financial costs involved in the project should be stated and a cost analysis should be carried out at the end of the project.

11   Check carefully all the safety requirements related to the project. *Make sure that if mains electricity is to be used for the project, the student checks with you before making any connections to a mains supply* and be sure that all transformer secondary coils are isolated.

12   Students should present all written and graphical material clearly and legibly. Every year students taking examinations lose marks because examiners and moderators cannot read some of the writing.

13   Present all numerical work clearly and legibly showing all the stages of calculation. This is essential if any mistakes are to be identified or calculations reworked.

14   A well-made good-quality prototype of the solution to the problem should be produced. A good criterion to use on completion is: can the student honestly say 'I want to buy it'?

▷

15 Students often evaluate their solutions badly, if at all. They should:
>   thoroughly test their solution;
>   check it fully against the design specification;
>   note any differences;
>   propose modifications;
>   obtain the opinion of others, including consumers and experts.

16 Give students guidance on writing their final report. This should include:
>   an attractive title page or front cover, and a leader page for each chapter;
>   an index with chapter titles and page numbers;
>   a clear and concise statement of the problem;
>   evidence of analysis and planning;
>   a full design specification;
>   appropriate photographs and sketches in 2D and 3D showing the various stages of progression (colour being used where appropriate);
>   a full report of the testing and evaluation;
>   appendices, bibliography, and acknowledgements.

Good grammar, accurate spelling and legible writing or typing should be used throughout. Check that the final report satisfies all the requirements of any applicable assessment criteria.

It is helpful to point out that the report should communicate to others all the relevant details about how the student tackled the project. It is a valuable document which the student could use at future interviews.

Other considerations and hints

1 Monitor the project progress at regular intervals; once every two weeks is recommended. Do not take the student's word that work is complete: insist on seeing it and check progress against the time plan.

2 Ensure that all students know the detailed criteria by which their projects will be assessed. Students should be given a copy of the detailed assessment scheme. Table 1 gives an example of an assessment sheet.

3 Make sure that if a student has produced an original and marketable solution to a problem he or she is advised about safeguarding it by means of the patent process.

4 Develop a questionnaire for students to answer which will give you feedback for *self*-assessment purposes. This can pinpoint successful and less successful aspects of the teaching.

5 Demonstrate to students previous good practice by having plenty of examples of materials on display. This will help to set and to raise standards.

6 Produce a developed strategy for progressing students from highly structured projects with few parameters to more open-ended projects.

7 When deciding on the accommodation required to run project work, due consideration should be given to its multi-disciplinary nature and problem-solving

▷

base. This will ideally require workshop and laboratory facilities, but if only one area is available it should be based in a general workshop area that can include a 'clean' area for activities such as electronics. If workshop facilities are not available, practical project work will be curtailed.

8   Build up a collection of reference material and make this available to students. A list is given in the Appendix.

Table 1   Example of assessment criteria

ASSESSMENT CATEGORY (% of total marks)	ASSESSMENT CRITERIA (Within each category the weighting for each criterion can be different)
PLANNING 10%	Understanding the problem and its limitations. Development of a strategy for solving the problem. Planning time, materials, equipment and skills.
COMMUNICATION 20%	Written work. Diagrams and drawings. Display of work and the report. Oral presentations.
REASONING 20%	Survey of previous work. Alternative solutions. Selecting the best solution.
QUALITY OF SOLUTION 40%	Suitability in meeting the design specification. Use of time, materials, equipment and skills. Originality. Conceptual difficulty. Aesthetic considerations. Potential for further development. Safety and environmental considerations. Efficient use of energy.
EVALUATION BY THE STUDENT 10%	Checking against the design specification. Modifications. Comparing with and canvassing the opinions of others. Cost analysis. Time evaluation.

Notes on the projects

The projects have been grouped into three areas as indicated in the *Contents* list. However, as explained above, the shorter projects can be extended into fuller projects, and the longer ones shortened or simplified by limiting the parameters investigated. The more complex problems cannot be simplified in this way as the problems set require a high conceptual level for solutions. These are more suitable for able pupils or for A-level students.

▷

The following symbols have been used to indicate the level of difficulty of each project:

■   an elementary project that could be successfully tackled by any student;

◪   a slightly more challenging project for average and above-average students;

☐   a difficult and complex problem for very able students, or for A-level.

Where background knowledge is required to find a solution, this has been indicated under the heading *Background work*.

Students' notes

Read these notes before starting your project. You will also find it useful to refer back to them at different stages during the project.

Organising your project work

When you have a problem to solve it is often tempting to try out the first idea that enters your head. Unfortunately, this is unlikely to be successful. It is much better to plan carefully and to follow a tried and tested procedure: the *problem-solving process*. Here are the stages of the problem-solving process.

1 *Breaking down the problem*

   To understand a problem fully, break it down into smaller parts. Imagine that you have to describe the problem to a stranger who has not come across this situation before. Your description should be detailed enough for him or her to go away and produce an idea for a solution.

   Now you need to think about the *limitations* that you have to work within — for example, cost, time, size, weight, materials, equipment available, and the skills that you have.

   Now draw up a complete *design specification*. In our problems we have helped you to do this by setting out some areas that you should consider. You should make a fuller specification. This should include all the requirements of your solutions and the limitations. Your final solution must satisfy all of the criteria in your specification.

2 *Gathering information*

   You will often need more information before you can tackle a problem. This will include particular information about the problem to be solved and possible solutions that already exist. You will need to find out about materials that you can use and their properties. Sources of information are your teacher, libraries, magazines. You may need to make visits or to write to companies. In some of the problems we suggest sources of information.

3 *Planning*

   Careful planning is essential. Before starting your project you must plan how you intend to spend your time, what materials and equipment you might need and possibly what skills you will need.

   It is a good idea to make a *time plan* listing all the jobs to be done and how long you think they will take. The total must, of course, be no more than the time allowed for you to complete the project. At the end of your project compare with your time plan how you actually spent your time.

4 *Alternative solutions*

   You should now begin to draw some 2D and 3D sketches of possible solutions to the problem. Then turn these sketches into a number of neater *isometric* sketches.

▷

At least three alternative solutions should be suggested. Label the important features of your sketches, the approximate dimensions and the materials to be used. Good annotated sketches can replace a lot of writing. You will find that using colour will improve your sketches.

5   *Choosing the best solution*

Each of your alternative solutions has to be checked against your full design specification. It is a good idea to use a table to do this. Table 2 shows an example. This will help you to choose your best solution. It is likely to include features from more than one of your alternatives.

Table 2

Design specification	Alternative solutions			
	A	B	C	D
Cost	3	3	1	1
Ease of maintenance	2	2	2	3
Low weight	2	3	1	2
Hard-wearing	1	3	2	1

Use a 1–3 scale:
        1 – solution hardly meets criteria
        3 – solution fully meets criteria

In this example solution B looks the best so far, except for 'ease of maintenance'. Solution D, however, meets this criterion well. Perhaps this feature of D could be included in solution B.

6   *Working drawing*

A working drawing of your best solution and a plan of construction are essential before you begin. These must include all dimensions, materials to be used, methods of joining parts together and so on. The working drawing should show front, side and top views of the solution. It is called an *orthographic drawing*.

7   *Constructing hardware*

Safety is extremely important when constructing hardware. Take note of all safety requirements when using tools and machinery, and of any safety notes in the project specification. *Electricity has many dangers and you must check with your teacher before using any mains electricity.*

8   *Testing, modifications and final evaluation*

When you have completed your solution you will want to test it fully and to evaluate it. A full *evaluation* is an essential stage in the problem-solving process.
        Your solution should be checked carefully against your original design specification. Use a table similar to Table 2 to do this. Note any differences

▷

between the original specification and your final solution, and propose modifications to overcome these. The modifications should be fully sketched and explained. You should also do cost and time evaluations.

Below is a list of criteria that you can use to carry out a full evaluation. Choose those criteria which are appropriate to your project. In some of the project briefs we have given additional guidance for evaluation relevant to that particular problem. With some problems you will have to do calculations to evaluate your solution.

All projects must be fully evaluated.

Some evaluation criteria

a   Does the solution work?
b   Does the solution fully meet the design specification?
c   What differences are there between the solution and your original specification?
d   Does the solution need modifications? If so, what?
e   How efficiently did the solution work?
f   For how long will the solution work? (This may need calculations.)
g   Does the solution need much maintenance?
h   Are spare parts needed?
i   What was the final cost?
j   Are there running costs?
k   Can the solution be used in all the specified situations?
l   Does the solution need transporting to the place where it is needed? Can this be done easily?
m   Does the solution look aesthetically pleasing in use?
n   Have you used materials efficiently? (This involves calculations.)
o   Does the solution use energy efficiently?
p   Does the solution have any effect on the environment?
q   Is the solution safe in use?
r   Have you used your time efficiently?
s   Have you obtained the opinions of other people to find out what they think of your solution? (These others should include those who may use the solution, and experts in the field.)

Keeping a diary

In order to keep a check on progress it is very useful to keep a diary. You will then be able to see quickly if certain activities are taking too long. The diary also allows you to check back to find out what you did in the last session. You can make a note of any ideas you have that may be useful later. An example of headings and possible entries for your diary is shown in Table 3.

As soon as you have decided on your project, start your diary. You will find it extremely useful when you write up your final report.

▷

Table 3 Diary of activities

Date	Activity	Time Planned	Time Spent	Notes
28.10.86	Produce working drawing	2 hours	2½ hours	One exploded view took longer than expected

Portfolio of drawings

At different stages of your project you will produce clear sketches and drawings. These must be kept together because they will form an extremely important part of your final report. Build up your portfolio of drawings as you work through your project and keep them safe.

Writing reports

A comprehensive report should be written about your project. Your friends, teachers and sometimes examiners will then be able to find out how you tackled your problem. You may have found an original solution to a common problem. In this case a company may take an interest in your report.

Your report must be written in a logical way and it should include the following:

a An attractive title page.
b A statement of the problem.
c The design specification, including all requirements and limitations.
d Background information.
e Planning – your time, materials, equipment, etc.
f Possible solutions – clearly sketched and explained.
g The choice of the best solution, and the reasons for this choice.
h The constructional details, including working drawings.
i Details of testing carried out and modifications made.
j A final evaluation and conclusions.
k A summary – a brief statement summarising your whole project.
l Appendices.
m A portfolio of drawings.

Your report should be neatly presented and it should read fluently. Any information that interrupts the flow can be included as appendices.

How your projects will be assessed

When you have completed your project you will want to know how well you have done. Someone, probably your teacher, will mark it for you. It is useful to know what criteria he or she will be using. Find out from your teacher how your project will be assessed. Make sure that you have covered everything in your report. The method used to allocate marks will give you an indication of how to divide up your time. Check with your teacher before you start your project so that you can plan properly. Remember, your teacher is a valuable resource: use his or her advice fully.

1 Lock it up! A child-proof medicine cabinet

The problem A medicine cabinet is likely to contain drugs that are harmful but attractive to young children. The door fastening must be easy for an adult to open but impossible for a small child to open. Design a suitable safe medicine cabinet.

Time 10–12 hours

Starting points

You should consider the following points when working out the *design specification*.
1 The door fastening must be secure.
2 Adults must be able to open the cabinet quickly – it will probably contain first-aid items.
3 Young children must not be able to open the cabinet. (You will need to carry out some tests to find out what young children can and cannot do.)
4 The fastening must be safe to use.
5 The fastening must be reliable and not too complex.
6 The fastening may be adapted to fit other doors, such as those of units under kitchen sinks.

Evaluation The solution should be fully tested. Ideally, it should be tested with young children. Other opinions could also be useful. Use the list in the *Students' notes* to produce evaluation criteria for this problem.

For the teacher *Background work:* Mechanisms; structures; electronics.
■   *Extension:* The solution to this problem can be adapted to other uses. The problem could also lead on to related problems on keyless locks and so on.

2 Overflow!
A bath-water alarm

The problem A busy father wants to make bathtime easier and he needs a foolproof adjustable device that gives an audible alarm when the bathwater reaches a pre-set level.

Time 10–12 hours

Starting points

You should consider the following points when working out the *design specification*. The solution must:
1 be easy to use;
2 be audible outside the bathroom (the warning may need to be given in a room some distance away);
3 be adjustable to any desired water level;
4 have a simple on/off switch;
5 be safe to use;
6 be cheap, in order to sell;
7 look good, and possibly be attractive to children to encourage them to have a bath.

Evaluation The solution must be fully tested and evaluated. Use the list in the *Students' notes* to produce evaluation criteria for this problem.

For the teacher *Background work:* Electronic circuits and construction techniques (the solution is likely to be electronic). Instrumentation and mechanisms may also be useful.
Extension: The solution to this problem could be modified, for example to allow adults to watch TV while filling the bath, or to save money by using less hot water.

3 Power stop: an electrical supply safety cut-off

The problem   When the mains electrical supply fails or is cut off, electrical appliances are often left switched on. This may be dangerous when the supply is resumed. An electric fire could come on again in an unoccupied house or room. Electrical appliances could be fitted with an automatic cut-off. They would then automatically be isolated from the mains supply if there were a power failure. Design and make a suitable cut-off device.

Time   10–12 hours

Starting points

You should consider the following points when working out the *design specification*. The solution must:
1   be safe to use, and conform to any relevant electrical safety standards;
2   be reliable;
3   fail in a safe position;
4   be easy to reset;
5   be cheap to make and fit, to encourage manufacturers to fit it.

Evaluation   Take care if you use mains electricity to test your solution. *Check with your teacher before making any connection to the mains supply.*

For the teacher   *Safety:*   Make sure that students are fully aware of the dangers and safe use of mains
electricity.
Background work: The heating and magnetic effects of electricity; a range of electromagnetic and electromechanical devices.

Keep it on the level: a ladder-levelling device

The problem   When you are using a ladder its feet must be level and secure. This is difficult if the surface is not level. Design and make a means of ensuring that the feet of a ladder are level.

Time   10–12 hours

Starting points

You should consider the following points when working out the *design specification*. The solution must:
1   be safe and reliable;
2   take account of the variety of types of ladder that are used;
3   cope with the maximum possible load, and incorporate a safety factor;
4   be easy to use and adjust;
5   be cheap;
6   be fitted permanently to the ladder or be interchangeable between ladders.

Evaluation   The solution should be fully tested under a wide range of conditions. Use the list in the *Students' notes* to produce evaluation criteria for this problem.

For the teacher   *Background work:*   Mechanisms; structures.

4

5 Tidy toys: a play/storage box

The problem   Design and make a box cleverly designed so that it may be used both as a playbox and as a storage container.

Time   10–12 hours

Starting points

You should consider the following points when working out the *design specification*.

1. The box should include a range of functions as a toy box.
2. The box must be able to store any accessories used for play and other toys: these should all be easily accessible.
3. Dimensions should be carefully considered.
4. The box must be attractive to children.
5. The box should encourage children to clear up after play.
6. A range of jointing and hinging techniques will need to be investigated.
7. Safety must be fully considered. Avoid projections and sharp edges, places for fingers to become trapped, and toxic paints.
8. Give careful consideration to the materials you use. The box itself should not be heavy.

Evaluation   Your solution must be fully tested and evaluated. Your tests should involve children of an appropriate age if at all possible: try a local nursery school or child minder. Use the list in the *Students' notes* to produce evaluation criteria for this problem.

For the teacher   *Background work:*   Structures; mechanisms; materials.

Keep your head down: a height alarm

The problem High vehicles often have to pass under obstacles – for example, low bridges on roads, and the entrances to warehouses. The driver needs a warning to tell him or her that the vehicle is too high to pass under the obstacle. Design and make a suitable warning device.

Time 10–12 hours

Starting points

You should consider the following points when working out the *design specification*.

1 The device must be adjustable. It needs to be set to the height of the vehicle or the load.
2 The device must give a clear warning *before* the vehicle reaches the obstacle.
3 The device must be reliable and give a warning if it malfunctions. The driver will be dependent on it.
4 The device must work in a range of conditions – day and night, rain, snow, different temperatures and so on.
5 The device must be protected from accidental damage, for example while the vehicle is being loaded.

Evaluation The conditions for testing your solution should be as realistic as possible. Use the list in the *Students' notes* to produce evaluation criteria for this problem.

For the teacher *Background work:* Optics; electronics; mechanisms; structures.
Extension: The solution to this problem could be modified to become a device for helping to manoeuvre large vehicles into tight spaces.

7 All fired up: measuring the temperature in a pottery kiln

The problem
Pottery is fired in a kiln at temperatures around 1300–1400 °C. It is important to have the kiln at the exact temperature for the type of pottery being produced. Design a quick and easy method of measuring the temperature from outside the kiln.

Time
10–12 hours

Starting points
You should consider the following points when working out the *design specification*.

1 The device must measure the temperature quickly and accurately.
2 The device must be easy to use and to read.
3 The temperature needs to be measured from *outside* the kiln.
4 The device must operate over the complete range of temperatures used in kilns.

Evaluation
Use the list in the *Students' notes* to produce evaluation criteria for this problem.

For the teacher
■
Requirements: Access to a kiln or furnace is required. Advice may be obtained from a pottery teacher.
Background work: Optics; electronics; a range of thermometric devices.

**Safety
in the kitchen**

The problem   Young children can often injure themselves by reaching up and pulling down
on themselves saucepans full of very hot liquid. What is needed is a way of
fastening a saucepan onto a cooker so that young children cannot reach the
saucepan handles. Design a device to achieve this.

Time   10–12 hours

Starting points

You should consider the following points when working out the *design
specification*. The solution to the problem must:
1   be suitable for a range of saucepans;
2   be convenient to use;
3   not damage the cooker or the saucepan;
4   have a quick-release mechanism operated by one hand;
5   be hygienic;
6   be made of materials able to withstand the temperatures involved, and be
easily cleaned.

Existing solutions to this problem consist of a guard around the top of the
cooker. This can be inconvenient and it can damage the surface of the cooker.
It does not always stop a saucepan from being tipped over.

Evaluation   Be careful when testing your solution; you do not need to use boiling water!
Use the list in the *Students' notes* to produce evaluation criteria for this
problem.

For the teacher   *Background work:*   Mechanisms; structures; electromagnetism. More information
about this problem and existing solutions can be obtained from RoSPA.

An open-and-shut case: automatic fume-chamber windows

The problem   A chemical fume chamber has a wide glass window that slides vertically. A chemist using the fume chamber often has only one free hand to lift the window. Because of its width the window tends to stick unless it is lifted evenly at each end. An automatic system for opening and closing the window would solve this problem. Design such a system.

Time   10–12 hours

Starting points

You should consider the following points when working out the *design specification*.

1   The solution must both open and close the window.
2   If the solution fails, the window must automatically return to the closed position, for safety.
3   The operator must be able to operate the system with one hand easily and quickly.
4   The window must move up and down smoothly.
5   Attention must be paid to the nature of the chemicals used in fume chambers.

Evaluation   The solution must be fully tested, under real conditions if possible. Use the list in the *Students' notes* to produce evaluation criteria for this problem.

For the teacher   *Requirements:*   Access to pneumatic systems will probably, but not necessarily, be required.
Background work: Probably pneumatics. Possibly optics; mechanisms; structures; electromagnetism; electronics.

10 The outer circuit

The problem Over the past few years the number of heavy lorries passing through a small village has increased due to the development of an industrial estate a few miles away. This has caused structural damage to the houses that are close to the road. Design and model a by-pass system to solve this problem, so that the lorries cause as little inconvenience as possible to local people.

Time 10–12 hours

Starting points

You should consider the following points when working out the *design specification*.
1   The scale.
2   A survey of the area and of possible routes.
3   The value of the land to be used.
4   Economics.
5   Environmental issues.
6   The suitability of the land to support the road and transport.
7   Residents' opinions.
8   Traffic information.
9   Safety.

Evaluation This will involve obtaining the views of local residents and local-authority departments to your solution. The criteria that you should consider can be developed by you in conjunction with the list in the *Students' notes*.

For the teacher *Requirements:* It would be a good idea to supply a local ordnance-survey map of the area.
Background work: Students should arrange to discuss the problem with the appropriate local government departments, and with local residents. Information on plant and animal environmental issues and on road construction will also be needed.

11 Avoiding the hot seat: safe seat coverings

The problem There have been several serious accidents in which fire has spread rapidly as a result of seat coverings that have caught fire and burnt. In many of these accidents, which happened in planes, buses and hotels, many more people could have been saved if the seat coverings had been flame-resistant. Design and conduct safety tests to evaluate the dangers of different seat coverings in a fire.

Time 10–12 hours

Starting points

You should consider the following points when working out the *design specification*.
1 The size of samples to be tested.
2 The measurements to be taken, such as the speed of flame spread, or the production of toxic fumes.
3 The safety and ease of use.
4 The range of materials.
5 The additives to materials.
6 The flame source, and its relevance to a normal situation.

Evaluation The evaluation criteria can be decided by reference to the list in the *Students' notes*. Some of the criteria could be built into the specification. Further evaluation could perhaps be done in conjunction with a local fire brigade.

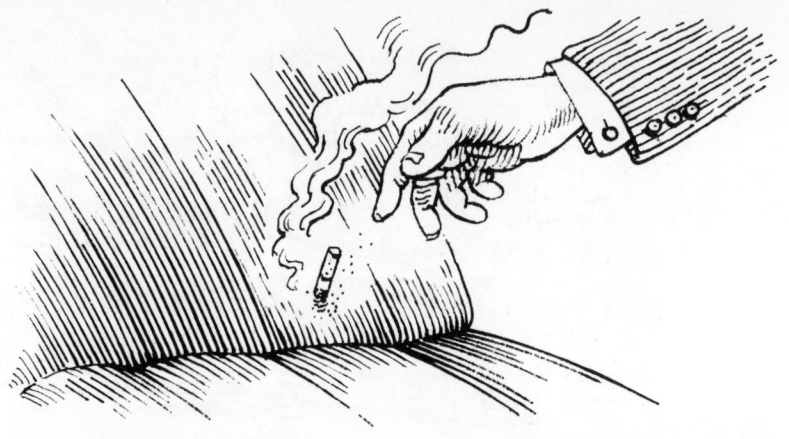

For the teacher *Safety:* The safety aspects of this project will need careful monitoring.
Background work: Fire and safety regulations; materials; materials surface treatments; technology and society. Discussions with local fire officers will prove very useful.

12 Electricity on tap

The problem   In a remote country cottage electricity is provided by a bank of rechargeable batteries. These have to be transported several miles to be recharged. There is a stream close to the cottage and the owner wants the batteries to be charged using the power from the flow of the stream. Design and make a model generator to do this.

Time   10–12 hours

Starting points

You should consider the following points when working out the *design specification*.
1   The scale.
2   The variation of the water force and rate of flow as a result of variations in rainfall.
3   The type of turbine.
4   The number and diameter of turbine blades.
5   The materials to be used for the device.
6   The generator.
7   The ways in which water will enter and exit from the turbine.
8   Safety.

Evaluation   How efficient is the turbine? Further evaluation criteria can be developed with help from the list in the *Students' notes*.

For the teacher   *Requirements:*   A suitable constant head of water and a generator.
Background work: Energy conversion; efficiency; structures; mechanisms; electricity; materials.
Extension: If a local stream is available this work could be extended to the design of a real turbine (a longer project).

13 Sailing – without water! A sail design for land yachts

The problem   A land yacht racer needs a land yacht that can be transported on the roof of a car. For competitions, the base of the yacht must be of a standard shape and size but the sails and the mast can be of any shape, as long as the surface area of the sails is correct. Design, and make in model form, the most efficient mast and sail design for the yacht.

Time   10–12 hours

Starting points

You should consider the following points when working out the *design specification*.
1   The scale of the model.
2   The surface area of the sail.
3   The mast size and shape.
4   The sail size and shape.
5   The ease of operation.
6   The angle of the sail to the wind source.
7   The stability of the yacht.
8   The likely wind force.
9   The materials to be used for construction and effect on them of weather.
10   Ergonomics.
11   Methods of securing the sail.

Evaluation   The solution should be fully tested using both constant and variable sources of wind, together with dry and damp conditions. A full set of evaluation criteria can be developed with help from the list in the *Students' notes*.

For the teacher   *Requirements:*   A vacuum cleaner, a rheostat and a spray should be provided.
   Background work: Energy conversion; aerodynamics; structures; ergonomics; stability and centre of gravity; mechanisms; materials.
   Extension: This could easily be extended to a major project.

Handle with care: efficient saucepan handles

The problem   Saucepans often have loose and burnt handles, and some handles conduct heat so fast that they are soon uncomfortable to hold. Design an efficient saucepan handle that is comfortable to use and that does not burn or come loose.

Time   10–12 hours

Starting points

You should consider the following points when working out the *design specification.*
1   The ergonomics.
2   The compatibility of the expansion and contraction rates of the handle and the holding-device materials.
3   The temperatures to be withstood by the saucepan and handle.
4   The conduction rate of the handle.
5   The range of temperatures that the hand finds comfortable.
6   Methods of fixing.
7   Materials.
8   Safety.

Evaluation   The solution should be fully tested under real conditions. The evaluation criteria should involve both quantitative and qualitative considerations. Further help in developing a comprehensive list of evaluation criteria can be obtained from the list in the *Students' notes.*

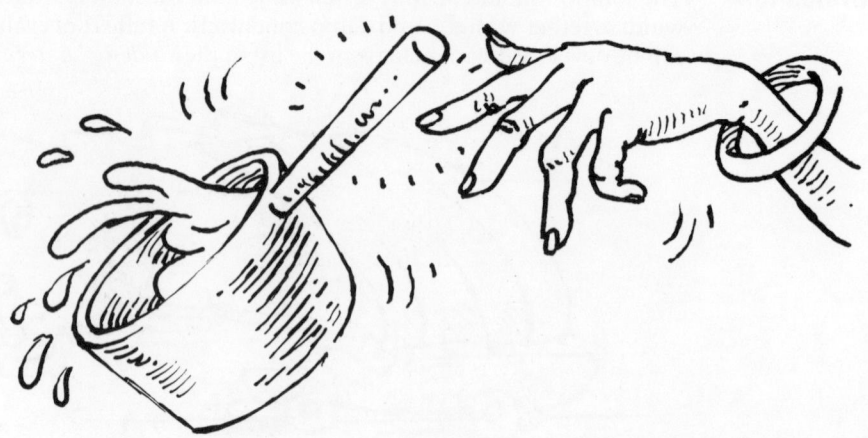

For the teacher   *Safety:*   It will be necessary to monitor carefully the safety aspects of this project.
■   *Background work:*   Materials; conduction; expansion/contraction; ergonomics; structures; fixings.

15 Look at it this way: aerial photographs

The problem The best way to see how a town or a set of buildings is arranged is to have an aerial view. This is useful when a new development is being planned, for example; and such views are simply aesthetically pleasing. Aerial photographs can be very expensive to produce if you have to charter a plane specially for the job. Design and make a cheap way of taking aerial photographs.

Time 10–12 hours

Starting points

You should consider the following points when working out the *design specification*.

1 The type and weight of camera.
2 The shutter control, to be operated from a distance.
3 The method of lifting the camera, and the force required to do so.
4 The height from which photographs are to be taken.
5 The effects on the equipment of height, temperature and water vapour.
6 The focusing and mechanism for alignment of the camera.
7 The materials to be used to construct the device.
8 The weather conditions that are likely to be encountered, and their effect on the equipment.
9 The motive power required.
10 Safety.

Evaluation The solution should be fully tested under real conditions. When developing your evaluation criteria you can obtain help from the list in the *Students' notes*.

For the teacher *Requirements:* If radio control is used, regulations regarding transmitter wavelengths will need to be observed.
Background work: Aeronautics (model planes, hot-air balloons, lift, controls, meteorology); effect of air temperature; structures; mechanisms; materials. Possibly electronics.

 **Aluminium/zinc alloys**

The problem

A local manufacturer of pressure-diecast components has been asked to make a number of intricately-shaped linkage arms in a zinc-based aluminium alloy with a tensile strength of 308 MNm^{-2}. This has given the manufacturer a problem as the zinc-based alloy he currently uses has a tensile strength of only 235 MNm^{-2}. Design, make and test a zinc-based aluminium alloy with a tensile strength of 308 MNm^{-2} to fulfil the manufacturer's need.

Time

10–12 hours

Starting points

You should consider the following points when working out the *design specification*.
1   The size of the samples.
2   The range and use of aluminium/zinc alloys.
3   The method of measuring the grain structure.
4   The method of measuring machinability.
5   The method of measuring tensile strength.
6   Safety.
7   The temperature of alloying and methods of cooling.
8   Methods of mixing constituent metals.

Evaluation

The various alloys should be fully evaluated for the qualities required, and a judgement made as to the alloy with the best overall qualities.

For the teacher
☑   *Background work:*   Materials (alloying, microscopy and grain structure, tensile testing); machining; casting.

17 Easing the load: a shopping trolley

The problem   People without transport can have difficulty in taking their shopping home from the supermarket. Design and make a model shopping trolley to help them.

Time   10–12 hours

Starting points

You should consider the following points when working out the *design specification*.

1   The scale.
2   Simplicity of use.
3   The ease with which the trolley can be taken up and down steps.
4   The carrying capacity and weight of the trolley.
5   Steering and brakes.
6   Safety when the trolley is used in poor light conditions.
7   Motive power.
8   How the trolley will be stored.
9   Materials.
10   Ergonomics.

Evaluation   The solution should be fully tested against a comprehensive set of criteria for which you can get help from the list in the *Students' notes*.

For the teacher   *Background work:*   Mechanisms; structures; materials; ergonomics. Possibly electromagnetics.

18 Blowing in the wind: a speed-and-direction indicator

The problem A private gliding club with a small airfield needs a clear and reliable indicator of wind direction and speed. Design and make a model to achieve this.

Time 10–12 hours

Starting points

You should consider the following points when working out the *design specification*.
1 The scale.
2 The distance from which the indicator must be seen.
3 The range of wind speeds that the indicator must measure.
4 Which colours are best for visibility.
5 The materials and weather conditions.
6 The serviceability of the indicator.
7 Whether or not conditions are to be continually recorded for reference.
8 The reliability of the indicator.
9 How fluctuations of wind, speed and direction can be alleviated to give consistent readings.

Evaluation The model should be fully tested using both constant and variable wind sources from many directions. Further evaluation criteria can be developed with the help of the list given in the *Students' notes*.

For the teacher *Requirements:* A vacuum cleaner, a rheostat and a funnel should be provided for this project.
Background work: Meteorology; the Beaufort scale; structures; mechanisms; stability; optics; materials; electronics. A visit to a local weather station and discussion with the officers responsible would prove useful.

19 Finding the spark: locating electrical cables

The problem   Electrical cables are located in the walls of buildings and are buried underground. For safety reasons it is often essential to know the exact location of these cables. Design a detector to locate such cables.

Time   20–30 hours

Starting points

You should consider the following points when working out the *design specification*.

1   Mains electrical cables carry alternating current (a.c.). The detector must be able to detect a.c.
2   The device must detect cables at different depths. This may need different settings. Does it need to indicate the depth?
3   The device must give accurate readings, though the accuracy may vary with depth. You must decide what accuracy is needed.
4   The detector must be reliable and safe to use.

You must be extremely careful when testing your device. *Mains electricity is lethal*. Check with your teacher before you begin testing.

You will need information on building regulations concerning electrical cables in houses and buried underground. This can be obtained from your local planning department.

Evaluation   Check your solution carefully against your specification. Use the list in the *Students' notes* to produce evaluation criteria.

For the teacher   *Safety:*   Work on this project will need careful monitoring.
■   *Background work:*   Electrical circuits; basic work on a.c.; house wiring in old and new houses; depth of underground cables; building regulations; instrumentation.

20 Congestion! Problems on conveyor belts

The problem   Cartons travelling at well-spaced intervals on a conveyor belt must sometimes be transferred to a second conveyor. This happens for example when a problem occurs during the packing of the cartons. The operator then needs to transfer the cartons to another area. Design and make a system to push the cartons at right-angles to the movement of the conveyor.

Time   30–40 hours

Starting points

You should consider the following points when working out the *design specification*.
1   The operator should have to push one button or switch only.
2   The carton should then be transferred automatically as it reaches a certain point.
3   The system should operate only when a carton is in the correct position for transfer.
4   Each movement must be complete before the next carton arrives.
5   The system should fail in a safe position.
6   The cartons must not be subjected to violent movement or shocks. They must not be turned over.
7   The system should not interfere with the normal operation of the conveyor or the packaging operation.
You may think of other points.

Evaluation   Access to conveyor belts may be difficult, but the system should be fully tested in as realistic a way as possible. If it can be tested on a conveyor, this is obviously an advantage. Use the list in the *Students' notes* to produce evaluation criteria for this problem.

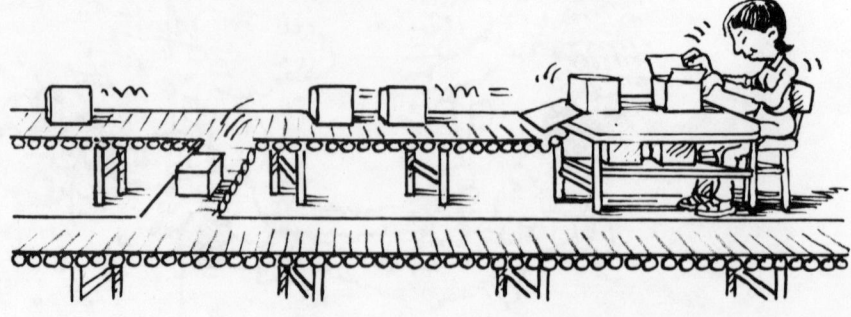

For the teacher   *Requirements:*   Access to a local factory using conveyors would be useful.
◢   *Background work:*   Probably pneumatic systems. Electrical switches; mechanisms; structures; optics; electromagnetic devices.

21 Helping the handicapped

The problem Old and handicapped people find many everyday tasks difficult. These include picking up objects from the floor, turning taps on and off, opening jars and cans, putting in and pulling out electrical plugs, and lifting saucepans. Aids could be made for all of these operations. Select *one* of these problems for your project. (If you can produce a versatile multi-purpose aid then do so, but this will be a much more complex problem.)

Time 30–40 hours

Starting points

You should consider the following points when working out the *design specification*.
1 The aid must be helpful: it should not make the task more difficult!
2 Many old and handicapped people cannot apply much force with their hands. You need to find out how much force can be applied. Calculations will then be needed in your design, so that sufficient force is applied to perform the task.
3 The final cost must be low enough for old people or health authorities to afford.
4 The dimensions will need to be carefully considered.
5 The solution must be reliable.
6 Give full consideration to safety features.
Other points will depend on the problem to be solved.

Evaluation When carrying out your evaluation, ask the opinion of people who would use the aid, and others working in this area. Use the list in the *Students' notes* to produce evaluation criteria for the problem you have set yourself.

For the teacher *Requirements:* Students will need access to old people; this may involve a visit to an old people's home.
Background work: Forces and levers; other mechanisms; structures; possibly electronics.

22 Hospital aid: an adjustable table for beds

The problem Patients in hospital beds need a table that can be used for many different activities. Design and make such a table.

Time 30–40 hours

Starting points

You should consider the following points when working out the *design specification*.

1 The bed must be used for a wide range of functions including: eating and drinking; reading books, magazines and newspapers; writing letters; drawing or painting; playing cards, chess and so on.
2 When doctors and nurses are treating the patient the table must not be in the way.
3 The table must not interfere with other equipment (such as drips) which needs to be attached to the bed.
4 Space in hospital wards is limited so the table must not take up too much space when not in use.
5 The table must not interfere with other functions and movements of the bed.
6 The table must be easy to place in position and to remove.
7 The table *must* be hygienic.
8 Safety must be fully considered – list all the essential safety features.
9 Costs must be realistic.

You may think of other considerations.

Evaluation When evaluating your final solution, check that all functions can be performed easily. (Find out the opinions of hospital staff, and people who have spent some time in hospitals.) A cost evaluation will also be needed. Think carefully about how you can check the hygiene and safety factors in your specification.

For the teacher *Requirements:* Access to a hospital bed, or a diagram of one.
Background work: Mechanisms; structures.
Extension: A hospital bed table for use with children; a modified bed to enable a partial invalid to get in and out more easily; keeping a person with back or respiratory problems in bed at a safe and comfortable angle.

23 Teaching aids for mentally-handicapped children

The problem Mentally-handicapped children are taught to know the parts of the body – head, arms, legs, and so on. This can be done using drawings and pictures. The children are asked to point to the relevant part on the drawing. Often the children cannot point accurately enough to indicate the correct part. Design a teaching aid to do this.

Time 30–40 hours

Starting points

You should consider the following points when working out the *design specification*.

1 You will need to undertake some research before you start this project. A local school may help you. Plan your research carefully; think out what information you require and how you will obtain it. (Your visits and research may reveal a different problem to solve. If so, talk to your teacher about it.)

2 Your solution must include feedback to the child. This should record success or failure and give the correct answer after repeated failure (you decide how many failures).

3 The solution must be safe – avoid sharp edges and corners, projections, electrical dangers and so on. Non-toxic paints must be used.

4 Your research will produce more points for you to consider.

Evaluation A full evaluation must be carried out. (Use the list in the *Students' notes* to produce evaluation criteria for your problem.) Make your tests as realistic as possible. It is much better if these tests can be done with the children who will use the teaching aid. Ask the opinions of people who work with handicapped children.

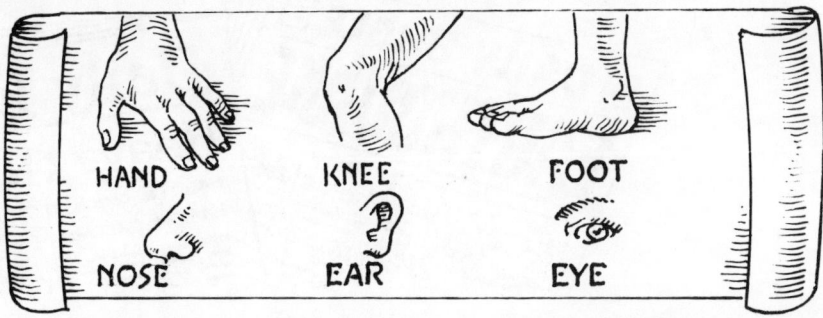

For the teacher *Requirements:* Access to a local school for mentally-handicapped children would be
■ extremely useful.
Background work: Mechanisms; structures; electronics.

24 An emergency shelter

The problem When there is a natural disaster, such as an earthquake or a flood, many people lose their homes. The emergency services need to provide shelter for these people. Design and make a suitable shelter.

Time 30–40 hours

Starting points

You should consider the following points when working out the *design specification*.
1   The shelter must be light, easy to transport, and easy to erect.
2   The shelter must be able to survive potentially hostile conditions, such as high winds, heavy rain, and extremes of cold and heat.
3   The shelter must provide facilities for sleeping and eating, and possibly for the preparation and cooking of food.
4   Consideration must be given to the following: the number of occupants; the basic dimensions; the type of roof and floor; sanitation; lighting, heating and ventilation.
5   Other basic supplementary equipment to be provided and packaged with the shelter must be specified.
You may think of other considerations.

Evaluation A full evaluation must take place; this should take account of all possible conditions. You should ask the opinions of people who have experience in this field. Decide what period of time the shelter will have to be used for: how will you evaluate whether it is possible to live in your shelter for this period of time? A cost evaluation will also be needed.

For the teacher *Background work:*   Structures; mechanisms.

25 Stretching it: a simple tensile tester

The problem A school needs a simple machine to measure the tensile strength of materials relative to each other. Design and make a cheap and suitable machine for this purpose.

Time 30–40 hours

Starting points

You should consider the following points when working out the *design specification*.
1 The size, range and preparation of material samples to be tested.
2 The forces required to break the samples.
3 The mechanism needed to apply the force.
4 The method of relating force to extension.
5 The method of holding samples.
6 Methods of measuring force.
7 Methods of measuring extension.
8 The ease of operation.
9 The accuracy required.
10 Safety.

Evaluation The solution must be fully tested with a range of material samples. Results should be compared with those obtained on a Hounsfield tensometer for the same samples. A full set of evaluation criteria can be developed with the help of the list in the *Students' notes*.

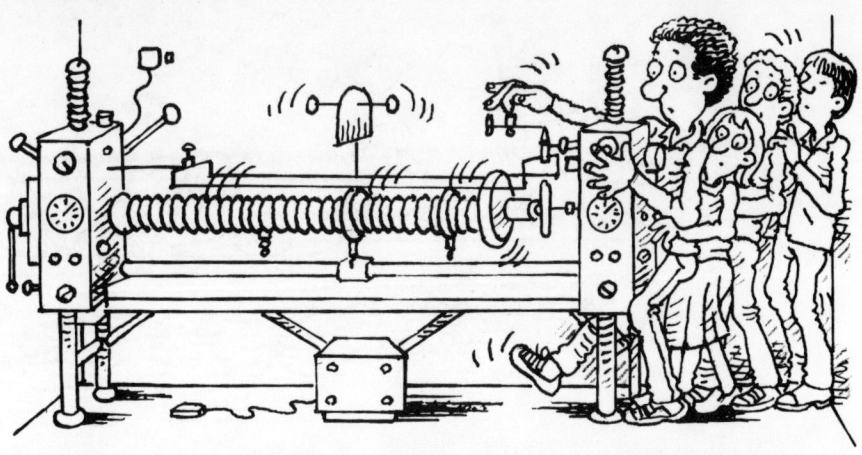

For the teacher *Background work:* Tensile testing; materials; structures; forces; mechanisms; amplification.
Extension: This could be developed for A-level. The project could be extended by including the effects of machining on tensile strength.

26 The long and the short of it: canoe footrests

The problem When school parties or other groups use canoes, they often waste time adjusting the footrests or attempting to fit differently shaped people into the canoes. Design and make a footrest for a canoe that is easily and infinitely adjustable within a maximum and minimum distance.

Time 30–40 hours

Starting points

You should consider the following points when working out the *design specification*.

1 The nature of material used and the structure of the canoe it is to be fitted in.
2 The greatest and least leg-length of the people using the canoe.
3 Appropriate ergonomic factors.
4 Materials: their weight and their liability to corrosion.
5 The cost.
6 Safety.
7 The time needed for adjustment.

Evaluation The solution should be fully tested by a variety of people (short and tall). Particular attention should be given to ease of operation and comfort in use. Use the lists in the *Students' notes* to produce evaluation criteria for your footrest.

For the teacher *Background work:* Forces and levers; mechanisms; materials; ergonomics; structures. It would be sensible to discuss the problems of canoe footrests with an experienced canoeist before starting.

27 Reducing your handicap: a foldaway golf trolley

The problem A bag of golf clubs is cumbersome and heavy to carry, but golfers need all their clubs with them throughout each game. Design, make and test a trolley to carry a bag of golf clubs. The trolley must be folded up and fitted into the golf bag for storage when not in use.

Time 30–40 hours

Starting points

You should consider the following points when working out the *design specification*.
1 The size of the golf bag.
2 The space inside the bag when it holds all the clubs.
3 The efficiency of operation.
4 The size of the wheels.
5 The materials: their weight and finish.
6 The ergonomics of the design.
7 Any applicable golf-club rules.
8 Safety.
9 The ease of cleaning.

Evaluation The solution should be fully tested under varying conditions (wet and dry, for example). Use the lists in the *Students' notes* to produce evaluation criteria for your trolley.

For the teacher *Background work:* Structures; forces and levers; mechanisms; materials. A visit to a golf club will be essential, and a discussion with the professional is desirable.

 **Stop the rot: the prevention of corrosion in mild steel**

The problem Mild steel is commonly used for a great deal of structural work because it is both strong and cheap. However, it is very susceptible to corrosion. A steel production unit wants to know what is the best coating to apply during manufacturing to reduce corrosion, and how this is related to the quality of the surface finish. Design and conduct suitable tests to answer these questions.

Time 30–40 hours

Starting points

You should consider the following points when working out the *design specification*.
1 The size of the sample.
2 The conditions that accelerate the corrosion of steel.
3 The conditions to which the steel is to be subjected when in use.
4 The range of coating materials to be used.
5 The grades of surface finish to be tested.
6 The methods of coating.
7 Safety (powder contamination, for example).
8 The method of holding.
9 The duration of the tests.
10 The need for pre-treatment of the steel before coating.

Evaluation The cost-effectiveness of the coatings must be fully evaluated for the total range of conditions and grades of surface finish specified. Further evaluation criteria can be developed with help from the *Students' notes*.

For the teacher *Background work:* Materials (corrosion, surface finish, surface coatings); metallurgy, microscopy; technology and society (safety and conservation).

29 Propellor power

The problem
A model-plane enthusiast wants to improve the speed of her plane for a competition which specifies that the engine size must not exceed 2.5 c.c. Design, make and test propellors to decide which one will give maximum thrust to a radio-controlled model aeroplane with a 2.5 c.c. engine.

Time
30–40 hours

Starting points
You should consider the following points when working out the *design specification*.
1   The power developed by the engine.
2   The effect of the propeller diameter, the speed of rotation and the balance.
3   The effect of the blade angle to the line of thrust.
4   The effect of the surface area of the blade.
5   The effect of varying the number of blades.
6   The test rig needed to measure the thrust produced.
7   The method of fixing the propeller to the engine.
8   Safety.

Evaluation
The various propellor parameters must all be fully tested on a standard rig with a standard engine to determine the most efficient propellor for the size of motor. A full set of evaluation criteria can be developed with help from the list in the *Students' notes*.

For the teacher
◪
Background work: Aeronautics (thrust, angles of attack, propellor design); structures; mechanisms; materials; energy.

30 Open wide!
A quick-release drill vice

The problem   On a production line it is important that all the operations are performed efficiently and quickly. If a component is being drilled, it must be held firmly in position. When the drilling is complete, the component needs to be released quickly. Design and make a quick-release clamping mechanism for this purpose.

Time   40 hours

Starting points

You should consider the following points when working out the *design specification*.
1   For safety reasons, the mechanism must not close too quickly and it must be released by a single operation.
2   The workpiece must be held securely.
3   A variety of workpieces will need to be held. The jaw opening should have a maximum of 200 mm and a minimum of 50 mm.
4   The mechanism can be mechanical, electrical/electronic, pneumatic, hydraulic or any combination of these. All services are available. A range of systems should be investigated.
5   The force required to hold the workpiece firmly will need to be found. Calculations will then be needed to determine certain parameters of your solution, such as the size of the pneumatic piston, the size of the solenoid, and the length of the levers. A visit to a local factory may be needed to find out some of the problems encountered on production lines, and some existing solutions.

Evaluation   Use the list in the *Students' notes* to produce evaluation criteria for this problem. It is important to obtain the opinion of others.

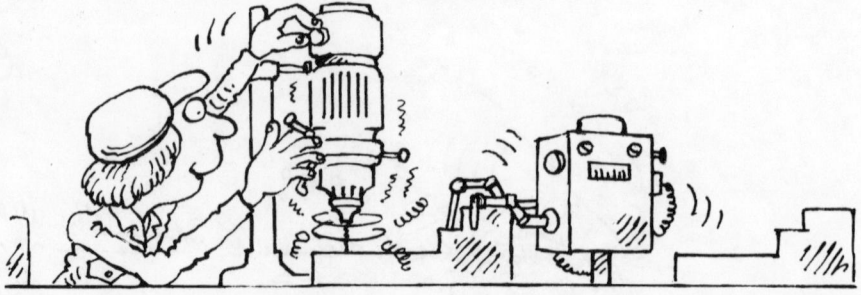

For the teacher   *Requirements:*   The solution may depend on the system available in school – whether students have access to pneumatic or hydraulic equipment. The solution will need to be tested on a drill.
Background work: A visit to a production line would be useful.

31 Radio-controlled glider

The problem   A gliding enthusiast needs a radio-controlled glider for a long-endurance flight competition. Design and make a glider that would be suitable.

Time   30–40 hours

Starting points

You should consider the following points when working out the *design specification*.

1 The aspect ratio.
2 The control surfaces and the linkages to the controller.
3 The tail plane.
4 The centre of gravity and siting of the controls.
5 The radio-control unit.
6 The aerodynamics of the body.
7 The strength-to-weight ratio.
8 The topography of the area where the competition is to be held.
9 The wind and thermal patterns for the area.
10 The maximum wingspan allowed.

Evaluation   The solution should be fully tested in a variety of weather conditions. You should produce a comprehensive set of evaluation criteria with the help of the list in the *Students' notes*.

For the teacher   *Background work:*   Aeronautics (basic flight principles); mechanisms; structures; meteorology; materials.

31

32 Hot water from the sun

The problem   A lady caravan enthusiast, who attends weekend rallies organised by the caravan club, needs to heat sufficient water to shower in her caravan. Design, make and test a suitable solar heater for the lady's caravan hot-water system.

Time   30–40 hours

Starting points

You should consider the following points when working out the *design specification.*

1   The type or types of caravan that the solution is to be used for.
2   The choice between making the solution fixed and permanent or collapsible and portable.
3   The volume of water to be heated.
4   The temperature required.
5   Safety.
6   The most energy-efficient heat-transfer system from the sun to hot water.
7   The possibility of circulating the water.
8   The orientation to the sun of the heat-seeking device.
9   Aesthetic and environmental issues (where is the caravan going to be sited?).
10   The ease of servicing and use.
11   The materials used for heat transfer, insulation and reflection.

Evaluation   The solution should be tested for its efficiency in converting solar energy into hot water, under varying solar conditions. Further criteria for evaluation should be developed with help from the *Students' notes* list.

For the teacher   *Background work:*   Energy; heat measurement; materials; structures; mechanisms;
◨ or A-level   optics. Possibly hydraulics; pneumatics; electronics; aerodynamics; technology and society. Detailed knowledge of caravans and caravan sites will be needed.
(When used for A-level there should be detailed considerations of control systems for flow, of temperature and automatic cut-off, together with sun tracking.)

33 Hotting up! A heating element for use in corrosive liquids

The problem   Due to the energy inefficiency of its heating elements, a chemical-plating company is commissioning the design of a more efficient heating element that can withstand the very corrosive solution used for nickel-plating. The company hopes that this will make its service more competitive, so that it gains further orders. Design, make and test such an element.

Time   30–40 hours

Starting points

You should consider the following points when working out the *design specification*.
1   The volume of solution to be heated.
2   The temperature range required.
3   How quickly the solution needs to be heated.
4   The power sources that are available.
5   A cost analysis against known alternatives.
6   The minimum efficiency required of the new element.
7   The chemical solution that the element has to withstand corrosion from.
8   Safety, including the flammability of solutions.

Evaluation   The new element must be fully evaluated for its resistance to the range of chemical solutions specified; and for its efficiency in converting power input into heat, and conducting this heat to the solution. Use the list in the *Students' notes* to produce further evaluation criteria for your element.

For the teacher   *Background work:*   Materials (conduction, composites, structures, corrosion);
□ or A-level   electromagnetics; control. A visit to a plating industry would be useful to give an understanding of scale.

34 Transport of delight: efficient transport networks

The problem The traffic division of a local council is concerned about:
1 how to get more people to use public transport, and so lower the concentration of cars and air pollution in town centres;
2 how to improve the energy efficiency of oil-based transport systems;
3 how to develop a cost-effective transport system for goods and vehicles, which will enhance the environment.

It is hoped that the council, after researching these areas, will be able to come up with a traffic system for the region that will integrate the various transport possibilities to give maximum convenience, energy efficiency and cost-effectiveness. Design a suitable traffic system to fulfil the council's hopes and alleviate their concerns.

Time 30–40 hours

Starting points

You should consider the following points when working out the *design specification*.
1 The geographical region to be considered.
2 The topography of the area.
3 The possible types of transport.
4 The demands for transport.
5 The energy efficiency of various types of transport.
6 Safety.
7 The social aspects of services.
8 The availability of transport-related services and energy sources, such as electricity and water.
9 Cost-effectiveness.
10 The incentives needed to change the public's attitude to the use of particular forms of transportation.

Evaluation It would not be possible in the timescale allowed to implement the proposed solution, but some qualitative evaluation could be conducted by means of consultation with professional transport managers. The parameters for such evaluation can be decided by reference to the *Students' notes*.

For the teacher
☐ or A-level *Background work:* Energy; technology and society; mechanisms; economics; advertising; electromagnetics. Meetings with a variety of transport managers and a study of regional topography will be necessary. It may be useful to contact 'Transport 2000', a national group for integrated public transport.

35 Wind power: a battery charger

The problem   An isolated cottage has no mains electricity. The owner is dependent on a 12 V power source for lighting and other low-power electrical requirements. The batteries supplying this power are heavy and need regular recharging. The nearest charging point is several miles away. Design and make a charging unit that will make use of the almost continuous windy conditions around the cottage.

Time   30–40 hours

Starting points

You should consider the following points when working out the *design specification*.
1 The current and power rating required.
2 The maximum and minimum wind forces experienced, and the average wind force.
3 Local planning regulations.
4 Siting and aesthetics.
5 Control and cut-out devices (regulation of output).
6 Cost analysis.
7 Safety.

Evaluation   The solution should be fully tested under varying wind conditions, to ensure that a constant output is possible. When the output falls below the required level the charger should be automatically disconnected. A more detailed list of evaluation criteria should be developed for your work with the help of the list in the *Students' notes*.

For the teacher   *Background work:*   Energy (conversions, efficiency, power); mechanisms (force, gear
□ A-level   ratios); electromagnetics; control (feedback, cut-outs); technology and society (local planning regulations); structures (forces, frameworks). Aerodynamics. An understanding of the relationship between wind and topography will be useful. Electronics may be used for control circuitry.

 # Portable centrifuge

The problem
A doctor in a Third World country has to cycle to see her patients. She needs a portable centrifuge to carry with her to test blood samples. Design and make such a centrifuge.

Time
30–40 hours

Starting points

You should consider the following points when working out the *design specification*.
1 The centrifugal force required to separate blood cells from plasma.
2 The control of the centrifuge speed.
3 The size of the specimen tubes.
4 The power sources available.
5 Ergonomics.
6 The ease of placing and removing specimen tubes.
7 Hygiene.
8 Safety.
9 Stability.

Evaluation
The solution should be tested to ensure that efficient separation takes place: this should be done with a substitute solution for blood. A visit to a local hospital for final tests would be very useful. Use the lists in the *Students' notes* to produce evaluation criteria for your solution.

For the teacher
☐ or A-level
Background work: Forces and levers; mechanisms; structures; materials; energy. A meeting with a Third World health organisation would be desirable.

③⑦ Wave power for boats

The problem   A local modelling club has organised a competition to design a radio-controlled boat, driven only by power harnessed from the waves in a 10 m wave tank. The boat must not be longer than 1000 mm or wider than 300 mm, and it must travel from one end of the tank to the other in the shortest possible time. Design, make and test a boat which might win the competition.

Time   30–40 hours

Starting points

You should consider the following points when working out the *design specification*.
1   The wave tank to be used, and the size of waves it can produce.
2   The motion of the waves.
3   The hull design.
4   Devices that can harness wave energy.
5   The materials to be used, and their resistance to corrosion.
6   The cost.

Evaluation   The solution should be fully tested under varying wave conditions. Use the list in the *Students' notes* to produce evaluation criteria for your boat and power source.

For the teacher   *Background work:*   Forces and levers; mechanisms; materials; structures; energy. It
□ or A-level   would be sensible to obtain books and other information on wave power and its measurement.
Extension: This could be extended to an A-level project by adding a greater level of quantitative considerations – for example, derivation of energy from waves.

 **Bull's-eye!**
Autoscore

The problem
A markswoman with a local rifle club is concerned about the cost of pellets. She thinks that it must be possible to make a target from which she could salvage pellets for re-use. She is also concerned that with conventional targets she has to move from her gun to a telescope between shots to observe the score, and she believes that you could design a target that would display the score electronically in such a way that she need not move her head between shots. Design, make and test a target that will meet these requirements.

Time
30–40 hours

Starting points
You should consider the following points when working out the *design specification*.
1 Methods of sensing.
2 Methods of displaying the score, and the clarity of the display.
3 The type of pellets being used, and the impact resistance.
4 The velocity of the pellets at the time of contact with the target.
5 Where the device is to be used.
6 The suitability of different materials.
7 Energy absorption.
8 Safety.
9 The clarity of the target.

Evaluation
The solution should be tested for the clarity of the display and the clarity of the target in specified conditions, together with the ability to re-use the pellets. Further evaluation can be decided upon by reference to the *Students' notes*.

For the teacher
□ or A-level
Safety: This project will need to be closely monitored to avoid accidents.
Background work: Optics; materials; impact forces; hardness; velocity; fluidics; electronics; energy; structures; mechanisms.

 **Biogas: a methane-gas plant**

The problem
A medium-sized mixed farm has a herd of fifty milking cows. The cost of heating water for washing udders and other operations is high. The farmer wants to reduce these costs by producing and using methane gas to heat the water. Design and make a methane-gas plant for his farm.

Time
30–40 hours

Starting points

You should consider the following points when working out the *design specification*.
1 The volume and flow rate of gas required. (This will involve calculations about the energy content of the gas and the amount of energy needed to raise the temperature of the water by the required amount.)
2 The pressure of the gas.
3 Storage methods.
4 Safety requirements (including regulations regarding gas storage).
5 The conversion rates of different animal manures.
6 The effect of temperature on conversion.
7 The control of the rate at which gas is produced and the time of production.
8 The materials suitable for the plant, in terms of their corrosion and strength.
9 The loading and cleansing of the plant.

Evaluation
Possible solutions should be fully tested under a variety of temperature conditions, and with the various types of manure available, to determine the most efficient solution. Further criteria for evaluation should be developed with help from the list in the *Students' notes*.

For the teacher
☐ or A-level
Background work: Energy (conversion, efficiency, conservation); structures (forces, pressures); biochemistry; technology and society; mechanisms; control. Possibly electronics and hydraulics.

 Safety in mountains

The problem   The weather on mountains can change very quickly. This can make conditions very dangerous for climbers and hill walkers. Changes in the weather can be predicted by changes in the atmospheric conditions, such as temperature and pressure. These changes can be rapid and small. People using the mountains need a reliable method of detecting these changes, which will warn them of any possible deterioration in weather conditions.

Time   30–40 hours

Starting points

You should consider the following points when working out the *design specification*.
1   The device must detect small rapid changes. You will need to find out more about these changes.
2   The device must make allowance for changes in altitude.
3   The device must be accurate and reliable.
4   The device must be hard-wearing and resist knocks and vibrations.
5   The device must be easy to read, or give a clear audible warning.
6   The device must be small and light so that it can be carried in a walker's rucksack or daysack, or strapped to a climber.
7   The cost must be realistic.
8   The device must work in a wide range of conditions.
You may think of other considerations.

Evaluation   Some points to think about: Did the device detect small rapid changes? Did the device work under all conditions? Was the warning clear? Did you try carrying the device all day? Did you obtain some expert opinions?

For the teacher   *Requirements:*   Access to information on weather, especially related to outdoor
□ or possibly   pursuits on mountains.
A-level   *Background work:*   Electronic/microelectronic circuits; construction techniques including a variety of environmental sensors; instrumentation.

41 Keeping a check on your plants

The problem   To grow plants successfully in a glasshouse a large number of conditions have to be very carefully monitored and controlled. These include temperature, light levels, moisture level in the growing medium, minerals in the growing medium, humidity in the atmosphere and ventilation. A commercial grower of flowers requires a system to monitor and control these conditions in her glasshouse. Design such a system. (You may choose one, several or all of these conditions for your project. Your teacher may help you to decide which ones.)

Time   30–40 hours

Starting points

You should consider the following points when working out the *design specification*.
1   The device must monitor *and* control the conditions.
2   The device must offer variable settings. The grower will need to change the conditions for different plants and different stages of growth.
3   The device must be fail-safe. A complete crop failure may result if something goes wrong. At the least a warning must be given before a disaster occurs.
4   The device must cope with the potentially hostile environment in a glasshouse. (Try spending an hour or so in one on a hot summer's day with high humidity!)
5   The grower is working to a tight financial budget. The solution must be as cheap as possible.
You may think of other considerations.

Evaluation   Some points to think about: Did the device successfully monitor and control the conditions? Did the device do this precisely enough? Did the device continue to operate over a long time period? Was the device cost-effective? A detailed cost evaluation may be needed.

For the teacher   *Requirements:*   A range of circuits will be needed (perhaps using microelectronics).
☐ or possibly   *Background work:*   Electronic hardware construction techniques. Possibly instru-
A-level   mentation; pneumatics; mechanisms; structures. Students will need information on conditions needed to grow plants (e.g. from rural-science or biology teachers).
    Extension: Looking after houseplants while on holiday.

42 Counted out! Automatic counting

The problem Fire regulations are very strict about the number of people that can be in a building or a particular room. A manually operated system for counting people in and out can be unreliable and tedious for the operator. Mechanical systems such as turnstiles are inconvenient and could be dangerous, blocking exits and slowing down evacuation in an emergency. An automatic system could overcome these problems.

Time 40 hours

Starting points

You should consider the following points when working out the *design specification*. The system should:
1 count people entering and leaving;
2 provide notice when the building or room is full (advance notice would be useful);
3 display the number of people in the building or room;
4 give no mechanical hindrance;
5 be reliable and safe;
6 not be obstructed easily;
7 be accurate, and able to take account of people walking side by side and in groups;
8 work in different light conditions and temperatures.
You may think of other considerations.

Evaluation A full evaluation must be carried out. Test your solution in as real a situation as possible. (Schools should provide plenty of opportunities for this.) Accuracy is essential; how will you evaluate this? The device must be reliable, so your tests should be spread over a realistic period of time.

For the teacher
☐
Requirements: A range of detectors.
Background work: Electronic/microelectronic circuits and construction techniques. Possibly pneumatic and optical systems.
Extension: Counting bicycles into school; counting cars into a car park (this could be extended to include a display of free parking positions).

43 Tracking the sun

The problem

For maximum performance from a solar panel or an array of solar cells, they must follow the sun. This enables them to receive the maximum amount of incident radiation. Design and make a device to track the sun.

Time

40 hours

Starting points

You should consider the following points when working out the *design specification.*
1   The tracker must have horizontal and vertical rotation.
2   The tracker must respond to a range of light levels and be sensitive to small changes of light.
3   The tracker must provide continuous or incremental movement.
4   The tracker must be reliable.
5   The tracker will be left out in poor weather and should be adequately protected.
6   The tracker should be fitted to the panel or array of solar cells. For this project initially make only a support for the tracker itself. If you have sufficient time you should mount the panel as well. In any case you should give some indication of how this will be done.
You may think of other points.

Evaluation

Testing must be carried out in a wide range of conditions. An infra-red lamp can be used to simulate the sun if necessary. Use the list in the *Students' notes* to produce evaluation criteria for this problem.

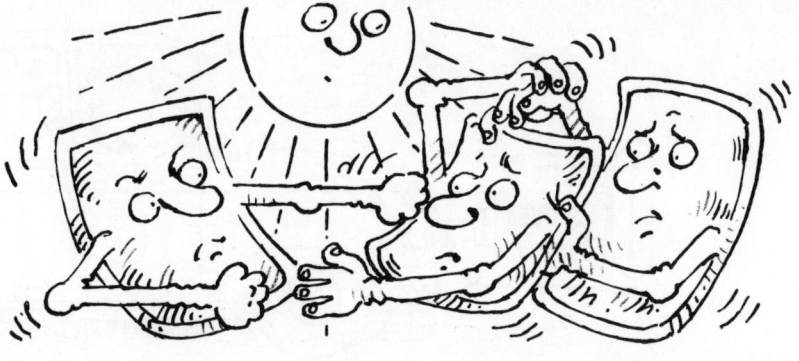

For the teacher
☐ or possibly
A-level

Requirements: Access to a solar panel or solar cells.
Background work: Electronic/microelectronic circuits and construction techniques (the solution could involve the use of a microprocessor); instrumentation.

 Motorway madness: a brake-safe monitor

The problem Driving on motorways is potentially hazardous. Although accidents are not common, when they do occur they are often serious because of the speeds involved. A major problem is that cars travel too close together, especially in conditions of poor visibility. Cars should be fitted with a device to warn their drivers when they are too close to the vehicle in front.

Time 40 hours

Starting points

You should consider the following points when working out the *design specification*.
1 Will the device simply give a warning at a pre-set distance? Is it necessary to adjust this distance according to speed and road conditions? Will it be manually or automatically adjusted? Could a device be attached to the engine to reduce speed automatically?
2 Any device must give a warning to the driver. How is this best done?
3 The device must work efficiently in all conditions: rain, fog, bright sunshine and so on.
4 The device will be in a hostile environment and subject to corrosion. It must be able to operate in these conditions.
5 The device must be extremely reliable.
Look in the Highway Code and elsewhere for information about braking distances and reaction times.

Evaluation Your solution must be fully evaluated. Use the list in the *Students' notes* to produce evaluation criteria for your problem.

For the teacher *Background work:*   Electronic/microelectronic circuits and construction techniques;
□ or possibly ultrasonics or optics; instrumentation. Sources: the Highway Code; motor manufactur-
A-level ers, the Royal Society for the Prevention of Accidents (RoSPA), motor-vehicle research establishments.

 **Growing plants
without soil**

The problem　To grow plants successfully on a commercial basis it is essential that they are given the correct amount of different nutrients and chemicals. The amount and type needed often depends on the stage of growth and on what size of plant is required. It is possible to grow plants without using any solid growing medium. This has the advantages of easy sowing and harvesting. Design a system to achieve this.

Time　40 hours

Starting points

You should consider the following points when working out the *design specification*.

1　You will need to research the methods of growing plants. Find out what conditions are needed, what nutrients are used and so on. Decide whether to concentrate on one type of plant or a range.
2　You will need to make a comparison of different methods, including conventional methods, and decide on the most suitable for the type of plants that you have selected.
3　It must be easy to sow and harvest the plants.
4　The plants need adequate support.
5　Ideally, the system should automatically monitor and adjust conditions in the growing medium. (This may be too difficult to attempt in the time available.)
6　The device must be cost-effective.
7　The device must be reliable.
8　A warning must be given if the system fails.

Evaluation　A full evaluation must be carried out. Use the list in the *Students' notes* to produce evaluation criteria for your problem. A cost evaluation will be needed. Any tests carried out must be over a realistic time period and in all possible conditions.

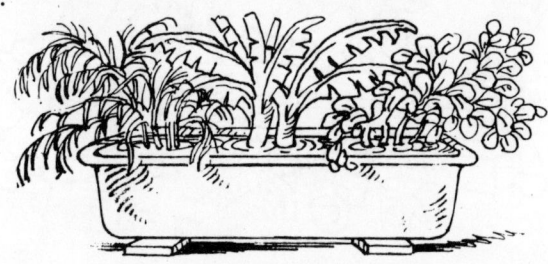

For the teacher　*Background work:*　Electronics/microelectronics; mechanisms; structures; instru-
□ or possibly　mentation; hydraulics.
A-level　*Requirements:*　Access to information on growing plants (biology and rural-science teachers and libraries are possible sources).

 **Up periscope!
OHP polariscope**

The problem   A teacher wants to show to a class of students the distribution of stress in an engineering component which is under load. To achieve this she needs a polariscope that can be used on an overhead projector (OHP). Design and make a suitable polariscope.

Time   40 hours

Starting points

You should consider the following points when working out the *design specification.*
1   The size of the OHP.
2   The limitations on the size of the polariscope.
3   The type of light source needed.
4   The polariser.
5   The analyser.
6   The quarter wave plates.
7   The method of holding components.
8   The method of applying stress to components.
9   Safety.

Evaluation   Testing must be carried out under classroom conditions and comments sought from teachers and students. To produce a comprehensive set of evaluation criteria for your project, use the list in the *Students' notes.*

For the teacher   *Background work:*   Optics; photo-elasticity; materials; polarised light; refraction;
□ or A-level   mechanisms; forces; structures.

 **47**

Going up!
Controlling a lift

The problem   To control a lift used for delivering goods to different floors in a warehouse.

Time   40 hours

Starting points

You should consider the following points when working out the *design specification*.

1   The lift is to be controlled externally. Controls are located on each floor used.
2   The lift must always be stationary at a floor level when the doors are to be opened.
3   The lift should move only when the lift door and all floor doors are closed.
4   The lift needs to be called from any floor.
5   The lift needs to be sent from one floor to any other floor.
6   It should be possible to open the floor door only on the floor where the lift is located.
7   The doors could open automatically or manually when the lift reaches the required floor.

It will be necessary to turn these decisions into a series of logic statements. You will have to build a model of the lift. Fischertechnic, Meccano or some other construction kit can be used for this.

Evaluation   Use the list in the *Students' notes* to produce evaluation criteria for this problem.

For the teacher   *Background work:*   Microelectronics and logic gates; mechanisms, structures. Possibly
□ or possibly   instrumentation; pneumatics.
A-level

 ## Stop that bike!
Bicycle braking

The problem   Bicycle brakes are often inefficient in bad weather. Design a safe braking system for bicycles, which is more reliable than the present systems. This could be designed to fit existing bicycles or it could involve a totally redesigned bicycle.

Time   30–40 hours

Starting points

You should consider the following points when working out the *design specification.*
1   The various weather conditions that the cyclist may meet.
2   The possible methods of braking and forces required for different speeds and conditions.
3   The inter-relationship of wheel and brake design.
4   The suitability of materials with respect to corrosion and erosion.
5   The forces imposed on the system by different people.
6   The sizes of bicycles.
7   Ergonomics.
8   Safety.
9   The cost.
10   The ease of maintenance.

Evaluation   The solution should be fully tested under varying weather and surface conditions, with both young and old people. Use the lists in the *Students' notes* to produce evaluation criteria for your system.

For the teacher   *Background work:*   Forces and levers; mechanisms; structures; materials. Possibly
☑ or A-level   electromagnetics; pneumatics; hydraulics; fluidics. A visit to an industrial cycle design unit could be useful.

Appendix:
Reference material

For teachers and students:

Schools Council Modular Courses in Technology (Oliver and Boyd)
Microelectronics: A practical introduction, R. A. Sparkes (Hutchinson)
Children Solve Problems, by Edward de Bono (Allen Lane)
How Things Work, Books 1 and 2 (Paladin)
Success in Electronics, by Tom Duncan (John Murray)
Applying for a Patent (The Patent Office)

It is essential to build up a collection of reference material for students to use when they are analysing problems. The above list should prove useful but is by no means complete. Teachers are advised to seek out their own sources of information.